Quidditch

by Martha London

The Greater World of Sports

SportsZone
An Imprint of Abdo Publishing | abdobooks.com

abdobooks.com

Published by Abdo Publishing, a division of ABDO, PO Box 398166, Minneapolis, Minnesota 55439. Copyright © 2020 by Abdo Consulting Group, Inc. International copyrights reserved in all countries. No part of this book may be reproduced in any form without written permission from the publisher. SportsZone™ is a trademark and logo of Abdo Publishing.

Printed in the United States of America, North Mankato, Minnesota
082019
012020

Cover Photo: Sergei Bachlakov/Shutterstock Images
Interior Photos: Phelan M. Ebenhack/AP Images, 5; Shutterstock Images, 6, 22, 25; Sergei Bachlakov/Shutterstock Images, 7, 20; Emmanuel Dunand/AFP/Getty Images, 8; Craig Russell/Shutterstock Images, 11; iStockphoto, 12; Christopher Capozziello/Getty Images News/Getty Images, 13; Dusty Compton/The Tuscaloosa News/AP Images, 15; Bonnie Vculek/Enid News & Eagle/AP Images, 17; Red Line Editorial, 18; Jack Taylor/Getty Images News/Getty Images, 26; Tina Fineberg/AP Images, 28

Editor: Melissa York
Series Designer: Melissa Martin

Library of Congress Control Number: 2019942110

Publisher's Cataloging-in-Publication Data

Names: London, Martha, author
Title: Quidditch / by Martha London
Description: Minneapolis, Minnesota : Abdo Publishing, 2020 | Series: The greater world of sports | Includes online resources and index
Identifiers: ISBN 9781532190414 (lib. bdg.) | ISBN 9781532176265 (ebook)
Subjects: LCSH: Quidditch (Game)--Juvenile literature. | Potter, Harry (Fictitious character)--Juvenile literature. | Fantasy role playing games--Juvenile literature. | Outdoor games--Juvenile literature. | Sports--Juvenile literature.
Classification: DDC 796.2--dc23

Table of Contents

CHAPTER 1
Seekers and Snitches 4

CHAPTER 2
Creating Quidditch 10

CHAPTER 3
Rules of the Game 16

CHAPTER 4
Quidditch Tournaments 24

Glossary 30
More Information...........................31
Online Resources...........................31
Index 32
About the Author..........................32

Chapter 1
Seekers and Snitches

February is cold in Ohio. Snow covers most of the ground. But that's not going to stop these players. The University of Toledo has a Quidditch team called the Firebolts. The seven players are squaring off against Michigan State's squad.

Fourteen players kneel in the center of the field, also known as the pitch. They close their eyes so they can't see where the snitch goes as he leaves the field. When the snitch has left the pitch and is far enough away, a referee shouts, "Brooms up!" The game has begun.

Quidditch players tussle over a ball during an April 2013 match.

Three rings stand at each end of the Quidditch pitch, serving as goals.

The seekers leave the field immediately, looking for the snitch. Keepers guard the three goals at each end. Dodgeballs fly through the air as the players run around with their brooms between their legs.

Chasers and beaters try to knock each other off their brooms. The chasers throw volleyballs at the goals at the end of the pitch. Each time a ball goes through the hoop, the scoring team gets 10 points. The crowd cheers with each goal. But the game isn't finished until one of the seekers returns with the snitch.

Players on the pitch wear jerseys and colored headbands to indicate their positions. No one has helmets or much padding, even though people are

All Quidditch teams are coed, with men and women playing together.

regularly tackled to the ground. Men and women play together on the same team, just as in the Harry Potter series by J. K. Rowling.

No one is flying around, but the game tries to keep as much magic in it as possible. This match took place in 2013. Some of the rules are still the same. But some have changed over time. Then, seekers and snitches could leave the field. Now all the action stays on the field where spectators can see it better.

Quidditch is a new sport. It has only been around since 2005, but the game has already spread around the world. As college students graduate, some of them bring Quidditch home into their communities. People are even talking about making Quidditch an Olympic sport. No matter what, Quidditch continues to be a popular sport on and off college campuses.

Enthusiastic spectators even dress up to cheer for their favorite Quidditch teams.

Chapter 2

Creating Quidditch

In the Harry Potter series, Quidditch players are witches and wizards who fly on brooms. The pitch has six high hoops of different heights, three at each end. Players on the two opposing teams have different positions. Three chasers score points by getting a ball—the quaffle—through a hoop. Each team's keeper tries to stop them. Two beaters aim balls called bludgers at the other team's players, trying to knock them off their brooms. The bludgers are magic and actively seek to hit people on their own. Meanwhile, each team's seeker hunts for a tiny magical ball called the golden snitch. It has wings and buzzes through

A set of Quidditch balls from the Harry Potter movies included large red quaffles and smaller brown bludgers.

the air, trying not to get caught. The game ends when a seeker catches the snitch.

In 2005, two students had an idea. They were freshmen at Middlebury College in Vermont. College can be stressful. The students wanted a distraction from classes, so they decided to recreate the game of Quidditch in real life. They formed a Muggle Quidditch club as a new intramural sport. A Muggle in the Harry Potter series refers to a person without magical abilities.

From the start, the creators wanted Quidditch to be a game that everyone could play. It was meant to be fun and a little silly. Magical balls like the snitch don't exist, so the

The snitch from Wizard Quidditch has wings and flies.

Middlebury hosted an early Quidditch tournament between several colleges in 2008.

snitch has to be a person in Muggle Quidditch. There is no actual flying, but players have to keep a broom between their legs at all times. This might sound strange. But it is a part of the wizard sport that the creators didn't want to lose.

That October, seven teams at Middlebury competed in the first-ever Muggle Quidditch tournament. Organizers found borrowed brooms.

Hula-Hoops served as goals. Players showed up wearing capes made of towels. Some even wore Harry Potter–themed costumes. The snitch runner was dressed all in yellow with a tennis ball in a sock hung from a belt.

It didn't take long for Muggle Quidditch to spread. By the fall of 2007, a World Cup for Quidditch was held between Middlebury College and Vassar College. Every year after that, more teams from other colleges competed in the World Cup. By 2009 the tournament had 2,000 people in the audience.

International Quidditch Association

In 2011 the first Quidditch match was played outside the United States. At that point, the International Quidditch Association (IQA) was founded. The IQA organizes tournaments around the world. It helps countries form teams. It makes rules for the sport. Many countries have their own local organizations, too. US Quidditch (USQ) is the organization in the United States.

Dressing up has long been part of the fun of playing Quidditch.

Muggle Quidditch celebrated its fifteenth anniversary in 2020. In a short amount of time, the sport has spread to nearly every continent. Quidditch is no longer just a sport for college campuses. Communities host leagues for people of all ages and abilities. Some of the rules have changed, but the goal of the game is always to have fun.

Chapter 3
Rules of the Game

Many aspects of Muggle Quidditch are similar to the wizard version. There are two teams of seven players. Positions include one seeker, one keeper, two beaters, and three chasers. The snitch is a neutral player. The snitch doesn't play for either team.

The seekers and the snitch do not play for the first part of the game. After the first 17 minutes are up, the snitch runs onto the field. At minute 18, the seekers follow. The seekers chase the snitch and try to catch the ball attached to the runner's belt. In the wizard version, the snitch and seekers

The snitch, *right*, wears bright yellow to stand out on the pitch.

The Pitch

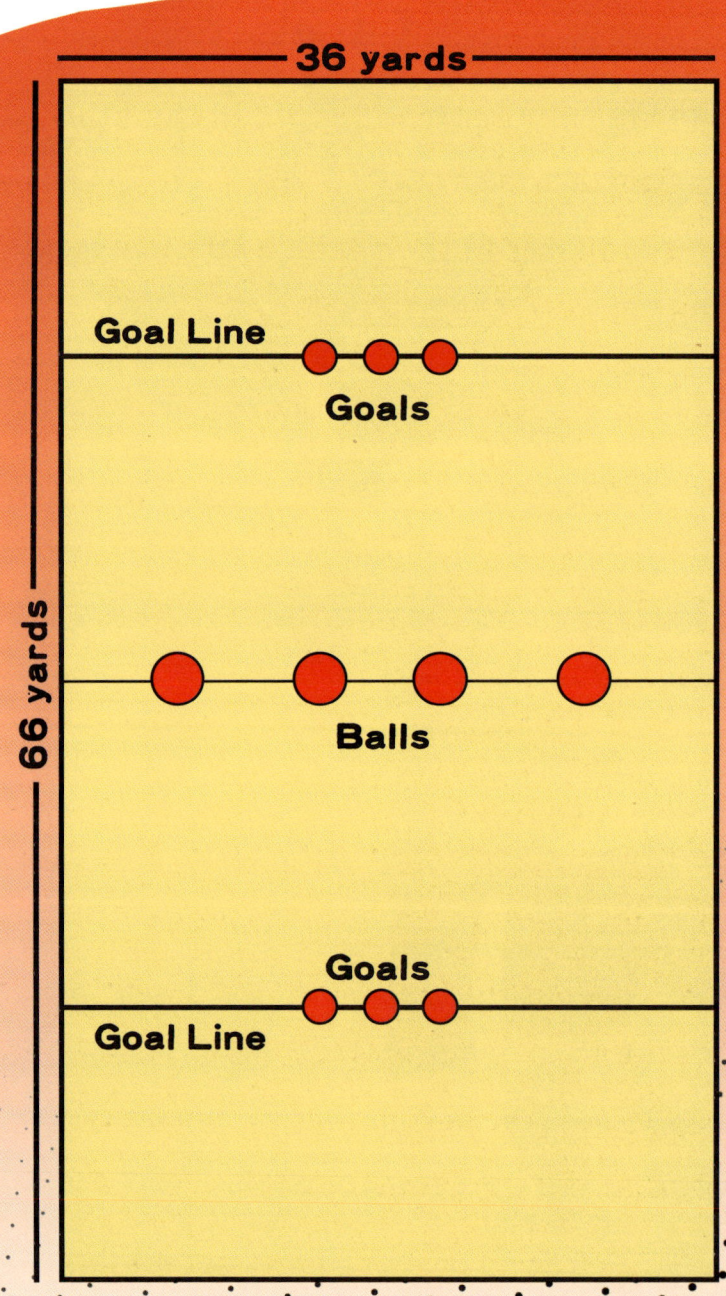

leave the pitch. They fly far from the audience. Early Muggle Quidditch was like this too. But in Muggle Quidditch now, people in the stands want to see the action. So the snitch and seekers enter the field later in the game and have to stay in bounds. This lets every person see all of the Quidditch players.

The keeper guards the goals. The three hoops are a little less than 8 feet (2.4 m) apart. Keepers want to keep the other team from scoring. Chasers attempt to score. They are the offensive players on the team. The defensive players are the beaters. Beaters attempt to distract or de-broom the other team's chasers.

In Wizard Quidditch, some of the balls have a mind of their own. But in Muggle Quidditch, teams use three dodgeballs and a volleyball. The dodgeballs are the bludgers. At the start of the game, the balls are lined up on the center line.

Quaffles are often volleyballs.

Players dash forward to grab a ball. Bludgers are wielded by the beaters. The volleyball is called a quaffle. The quaffle is the ball for scoring goals.

Chasers try to throw the quaffle through the hoops that the keeper is guarding.

Originally the goals were made from Hula-Hoops. Some community teams still use them. Bigger teams and many college teams use sturdier hoops made out of plastic pipes. Just as in magical Quidditch, the three goals are at different heights. But all of them are worth the same ten points.

Muggle Quidditch is full contact, like the wizard version. Tackling, or wrapping, is allowed. Players may only tackle a player if that person has a ball in hand. During a wrap, the player must maintain one hand on his or her broom at all times. Seekers are not allowed to tackle the snitch.

The beaters who throw bludgers hope to hit the other team's players. When players are hit by bludgers, they must dismount their brooms. Before they can return to the game, they must run back and touch one of their team's hoops. This mimics the time it would take for a player to remount their broom in a magical Quidditch game.

With tackling and no protective pads, playing Quidditch can result in injuries.

The creators of Muggle Quidditch also kept the sport coed. People of all genders are welcome to play on the same team. Official teams have rules to keep genders balanced.

Games last until the snitch is captured. This ends the game. Capturing the snitch is worth 30 points. But the team that gets the golden snitch might not win the match. In the end, the team with the most points wins.

Title 9¾

Title 9¾ gets its name from Platform 9¾, where wizard students board the train to Hogwarts each fall. But Title 9¾ doesn't have anything to do with magic. It is a gender-equality rule. It is also the branch of USQ that makes sure rules and policies prevent gender discrimination on Muggle Quidditch teams. One way it does this is through the Gender Maximum Rule. This rule states that at least two players on every team must be a different gender than two other players.

Chapter 4
Quidditch Tournaments

Quidditch is played on every continent except Antarctica. USQ governs the sport in the United States. It publishes standard rules, certifies referees and snitches, hosts championships, and is working to expand the sport throughout the country. The IQA estimates that 8,000 to 9,000 people participate in the sport. These players make up 600 teams across 40 different countries.

The IQA hosts massive international tournaments. The World Cup is held every two years. In 2018, the Cup had 29 competing teams. Thousands of people got tickets to see the teams

The 2018 Quidditch World Cup was held in Italy.

face off. The United States beat Belgium in the finals.

During the off years the IQA also hosts continental games. As of 2019, there were European Games and Pan-American Games. The Pan-American Games feature North, Central, and South American teams. As the sport of Quidditch continues to grow, it is likely that the IQA will host other continental games.

But the IQA isn't the only organization hosting tournaments. Quidditch was created so it could be played by everyone. Local Quidditch organizations hold regional tournaments. These tournaments generally bring together Quidditch leagues from several different states.

On a lower level than that are recreational and community club teams, as well as college clubs. The collegiate Quidditch league hosts its

Teams from London, England, faced off during the city's Crumpet Cup tournament, one of many regional tournaments held around the globe.

The IQA hosts events teaching kids how to play Quidditch.

own World Cup in the United States. Quidditch is becoming more popular for younger players, too. USQ provides adapted rules for younger players and also helps adult teams reach out to kids at summer camps and afterschool programs.

More serious teams practice multiple times per week. But a person doesn't have to be the next Harry Potter to have fun playing Muggle Quidditch. No matter what level players are at, or even whether players have read the Harry Potter series, all are welcome to join a Quidditch team.

Major League Quidditch

In 2015 a long-time Quidditch player and a group of friends created Major League Quidditch. MLQ teams throughout the United States and Canada are divided into three regions, East, North, and South, each with five teams. MLQ teams have a regular season. It begins June 1 and ends August 30. The teams play 12 games in each regular season against teams in their division. The postseason is interdivision, with the top 12 teams overall competing for the championship.

Glossary

campus
The buildings and property of a school.

discrimination
The unfair treatment of a person because of a quality such as gender or race.

dismount
Get down from.

interdivision
Played by teams that are from multiple regions.

intramural
Played by teams that are all from the same school.

neutral
Not loyal to a specific team.

pitch
The field where Quidditch matches take place.

More Information

BOOKS

Decker, Michael. *Dodgeball*. Minneapolis, MN: Abdo Publishing, 2020.

Lemke, Donald. *Harry Potter Quidditch at Hogwarts: The Player's Guide*. Philadelphia: Running Press, 2020.

Whisp, Kennilworthy. *Quidditch through the Ages*. New York: Arthur A. Levine, 2001.

ONLINE RESOURCES

To learn more about Quidditch, please visit **abdobooklinks.com** or scan this QR code. These links are routinely monitored and updated to provide the most current information available.

Index

beaters, 7, 10, 16, 19–22
bludgers, 10, 19–21
brooms, 4–7, 10, 13, 19, 21–22

changes to rules, 9, 19
chasers, 7, 10, 16, 19, 21
children's teams, 28
coed, 9, 23
college teams, 9, 12–15, 21, 28
continental games, 27
costumes, 14

goals, 6–7, 10, 14, 19–21

headbands, 7

International Quidditch Association, 14, 24–27

jerseys, 7

keepers, 6, 10, 16, 19, 21

leagues, 15, 27–28

Major League Quidditch, 28

pitch, 4, 7, 10, 19

quaffle, 10, 20–21

referees, 4, 24
Rowling, J. K., 9

scoring points, 7, 10, 19–20, 23
seekers, 6–9, 10–12, 16–19, 22
snitch, 4–9, 10–14, 16–19, 21, 23, 24

tackling, 7–9, 21
Title 9¾, 23
tournaments, 13–14, 24–27

US Quidditch, 14, 23, 24, 28

Wizard Quidditch, 10–13, 16–19, 21–22
World Cup, 14, 24–27, 28

About the Author

Martha London writes books for young readers full time. When she isn't writing, you can find her hiking in the Minnesota woods.